# THE BOOK OF GREAT
## *Jazz*

Project Manager: Tony Esposito
Book Design: Jorge Paredes

# Contents

# BODY AND SOUL

Words by
EDWARD HEYMAN, ROBERT SOUR
and FRANK EYTON

Music by
JOHNNY GREEN

Body and Soul - 3 - 1

# A SHINE ON YOUR SHOES

Words by
HOWARD DIETZ

Music by
ARTHUR SCHWARTZ

Don't you be a good for noth-in', Nev-er 'mount to noth-in', Hang-in' round the cor-ners! Can't you see you nev-er will be get-tin' an-y-where.

# YOU'RE THE TOP

Words and Music by
COLE PORTER

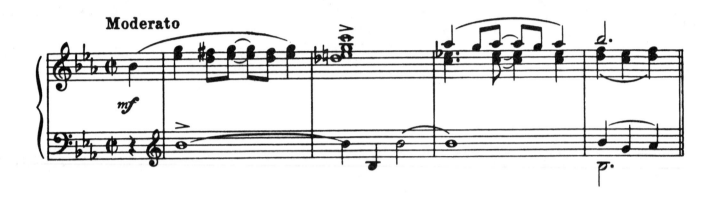

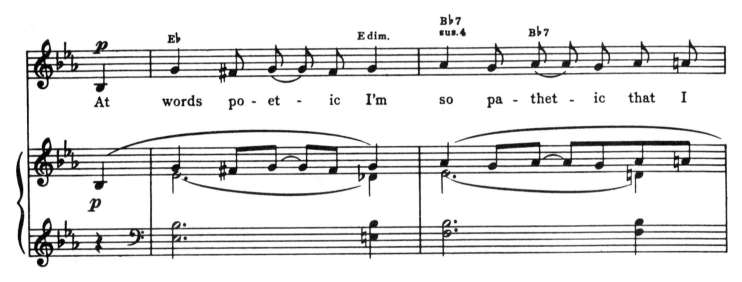

At words po-et-ic I'm so pa-thet-ic that I

al-ways have found it best,___ In-stead of get-ting 'em off___ my

You're the Top - 5 - 1

14

REFRAIN

# DAY IN - DAY OUT

Words by
JOHNNY MERCER

Music by
RUBE BLOOM

# AM I BLUE?

*On with the Show*

Words by
GRANT CLARKE

Music by
HARRY AKST

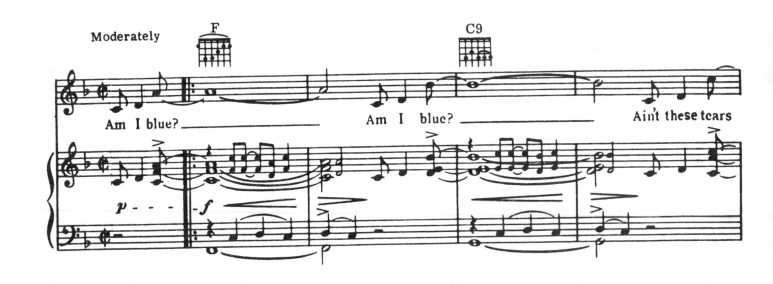

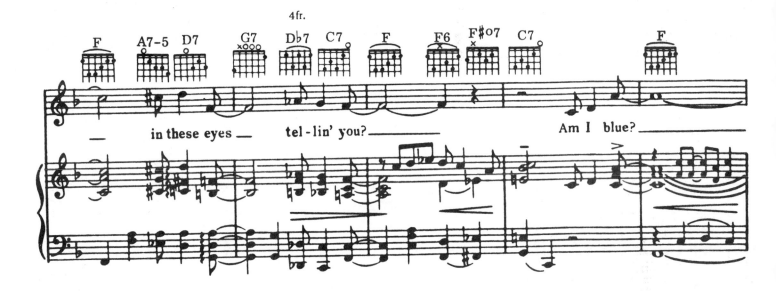

# ZING! WENT THE STRINGS OF MY HEART

Words and Music by
JAMES F. HANLEY

In per-fect har-mo-ny, — Zing! went the strings of my heart. —

Your eyes made skies seem blue a-gain, What else could I do a-gain, But

keep re-peat-ing through a-gain "I love you, love you!"

# ANYTHING GOES
## From The Musical "ANYTHING GOES"

Words and Music by
COLE PORTER

Anything Goes - 4 - 1

day_____ An - y shock they should try to stem,___

'Stead of land-ing on Ply-mouth Rock, Ply-mouth Rock would land on them.___

**REFRAIN**

In old - en days a glimpse of stock-ing Was looked on as some-thing shock-

ing, Now heav - en knows,_____ An - y - thing goes.___

# WHAT IS THIS THING CALLED LOVE?

Words and Music by
COLE PORTER

I was a hum-drum per-son, Lead-ing a life a part, When love flew in through my win-dow wide And

You gave me days of sun-shine, You gave me nights of cheer, You made my life an en-chant-ed dream, Till

What Is This Thing Called Love? - 4 - 1

What Is This Thing Called Love? - 4 - 4

# APRIL IN PARIS

Words by
**E.Y. HARBURG**
*French Version by*
**EMELIA RENAUD**

Music by
**VERNON DUKE**

April in Paris - 4 - 1

# TUXEDO JUNCTION

Words by
BUDDY FEYNE

Music by
ERSKINE HAWKINS, WILLIAM JOHNSON
and JULIAN DASH

# LOVE FOR SALE

Words and Music by
COLE PORTER

Love for Sale - 3 - 1

# TOO CLOSE FOR COMFORT

Words and Music by
JERRY BOCK, LARRY HOLOFCENER
and GEORGE DAVID WEISS

# AUTUMN NOCTURNE

Words by
KIM GANNON

Music by
JOSEF MYROW

**Slow Indigo tempo**

When au-tumn sings her lull-a-by___ And green leaves turn to gold _____ Then I re-mem-ber last Sep-tem-ber you and I said good-

# THOU SWELL
### (From "A Connecticut Yankee")

Words by LORENZ HART

Music by RICHARD RODGERS

Thou Swell - 2 - 1

# BLUES IN THE NIGHT
## (My Mama Done Tol' Me)

*Blues in the Night*

Words by
JOHNNY MERCER

Music by
HAROLD ARLEN

Blues in the Night - 4 - 1

# TAKING A CHANCE ON LOVE

Words by
JOHN LATOUCHE and
TED FETTER

Music by
VERNON DUKE

Here I go a-gain___ I hear those trum-pets blow a-gain___
Here I come a-gain___ I'm gon-na make things hum a-gain___
Here I slip a-gain___ a-bout to take that tip a-gain___

all a-glow a-gain___ Tak-ing A Chance On Love
act-ing dumb a-gain___ Tak-ing A Chance On Love
got my grip a-gain___ Tak-ing A Chance On Love

Here I slide a-gain___ a-bout to take that ride a-gain___
Here I stand a-gain___ a-bout to beat the band a-gain___
Now I prove a-gain___ that I can make life move a-gain___

star-ry-eyed a-gain___ Tak-ing A Chance On Love.   I
feel-ing grand a-gain___ Tak-ing A Chance On Love.   I
in the groove a-gain___ Tak-ing A Chance On Love   I

Taking A Chance On Love - 2 - 1

# MOOD INDIGO

Words and Music by
DUKE ELLINGTON, IRVING MILLS
and ALBANY BIGARD

# MY KIND OF TOWN
## (Chicago Is)

Words by
SAMMY CAHN

Music by
JAMES VAN HEUSEN

My Kind of Town - 5 - 1

64

CHORUS (*nice walking style*)

All the things Chi - ca-go is to me. Gee! It's

My KIND OF TOWN Chi - ca - go is,

My KIND OF TOWN Chi - ca - go is,

My kind of peo - ple, too, _____
My kind of razz - ma - tazz, _____

*) Any city name of three syllables can replace Chicago; such as Manhattan, Las Vegas, etc.

My Kind of Town - 5 - 2

# BUGLE CALL RAG

Words and Music by
JACK PETTIS, BILLY MEYERS
and ELMER SCHOEBEL

Bugle Call Rag - 2 - 1

Bugle Call Rag - 2 - 2

# THAT'S ALL

Words and Music by
ALAN BRANDT and BOB HAYMES

# 'ROUND MIDNIGHT

Words by
BERNIE HANIGHEN

Music by
COOTIE WILLIAMS and THELONIOUS MONK

'Round Midnight - 6 - 1

# CARAVAN

By
DUKE ELLINGTON, IRVING MILLS
and JUAN TIZOL

Caravan - 4 - 1

# EMBRACEABLE YOU

Music and Lyrics by
GEORGE GERSHWIN
and IRA GERSHWIN

# TAKE 6

By
DAVID BENOIT

*Nominee, Best Song, 1955*

# SOMETHING'S GOTTA GIVE

*Daddy Long Legs*

Words and Music by
JOHNNY MERCER

Something's Gotta Give - 4 - 1

Something's Gotta Give - 4 - 4

# CHATTANOOGA CHOO CHOO

Lyrics by
MACK GORDON

Music by
HARRY WARREN

Chattanooga Choo Choo - 4 - 1

# STAR DUST

by MITCHELL PARISH
*French Translation by*
YVETTE BARUCH

Music by
HOAGY CARMICHAEL

Some- times I won- der why I spend the lone- ly night
*Sou - vent le si - lence de la nuit ré - pète ton nom*

Dream- ing of a song? The mel - o - dy haunts my rev-er-ie, And I am once a - gain with
*Comme un - e chan-son, Sa mél - o - die hante ma rêv-er-ie, Mon rêve me trans-porte dans les*

you,____ When our love was new, and each kiss an in-spir-a - tion.____
*bras____ Quand l'a - mour fût jeune, et chaque bai - ser in-spir-a - tion,____*

But that was long a - go: now my con-so-la - tion is in the star dust of a
*Les ann - ées sont pass-ées et ma con-so-la - tion s't - lève à l'é - toile d'une chan-*

Star Dust - 2 - 1

# LET'S DO IT
## (Let's Fall in Love)

Words and Music by
COLE PORTER

Let's Do It - 5 - 1

# I THOUGHT ABOUT YOU

Words by
JOHNNY MERCER

Music by
JAMES VAN HEUSEN

# CUTE

Words by
STANLEY STYNE

Music by
NEAL HEFTI

Moderately, with a swinging beat

Cute - 2 - 1

# COME FLY WITH ME

Words by
SAMMY CAHN

Music by
JAMES VAN HEUSEN

Come Fly With Me - 4 - 1

108

# SWEET GEORGIA BROWN

Words and Music by
BEN BERNIE, MACEO PINKARD
and KENNETH CASEY

She just got here yes-ter-day,___
Brown-skin Gals you'll get the blues,___

Things are hot here now they say,___ There's ___ a big change in
Brown-skin Pals you'll sure-ly lose,___ And ___ there's but one ex-

Sweet Georgia Brown - 4 - 1

Sweet Georgia Brown - 4 - 4

# DON'T GET AROUND MUCH ANYMORE

Lyric by
BOB RUSSELL

Music by
DUKE ELLINGTON

Verse:

When I'm not play-ing sol-i-taire___ I take a book down from the shelf And what with pro-grams on the air I keep pret-ty much to my-self.

Chorus:

Missed the Sat-ur-day dance     Heard they crowd-ed the

Don't Get Around Much Anymore - 3 - 1

more at ease\_\_\_\_\_ but nev - er - the - less\_\_\_\_\_

why stir up mem - o - ries\_\_\_\_\_ Been in - vit - ed on dates

Might have gone but what for Aw - f'lly dif - f'rent with - out\_\_\_\_\_ you\_

Don't Get A - round Much An - y More Missed the Sat - ur - day More.

# SKYLARK

Words by
JOHNNY MERCER

Music by
HOAGY CARMICHAEL

Skylark - 3 - 1

118

Skylark - 3 - 3

# FASCINATING RHYTHM

Music and Lyrics by
GEORGE GERSHWIN and IRA GERSHWIN

Got a lit-tle rhy-thm, A rhy-thm, a rhy-thm That pit-a-pats through my brain. So darn per-sis-tent, The day is-n't dis-tant When it-'ll drive me in-sane. Comes in the morn-ing With-

Fascinating Rhythm - 4 - 1

out an-y warn-ing, And hangs a-round_all day. I'll have to sneak up to it,

Some-day, and speak up to it, I hope it list-ens when I say:

**REFRAIN**

"Fas-ci-nat-ing Rhy-thm You've got me on the go! Fas-ci - nat-ing Rhy-thm I'm all a -

qui - ver. What a mess you're mak-ing! The neigh-bors want to know why I'm

# SOLITUDE

Tune Uke
A D F♯ B
Put Capo on 1st Fret

By
DUKE ELLINGTON, EDDIE DE LANGE
and IRVING MILLS

VOICE

Slowly, *(with expression)*

In my SOL-I-TUDE___ you haunt me With

re-ver-ies___ of days gone by ___ In my SOL-I-TUDE___ you

taunt me With mem-o-ries___ that nev-er die ___ I

Solitude - 2 - 1

# THEME FROM "THE FOX"

By
LALO SCHIFRIN

**Moderately slow**

Theme from "The Fox" - 2 - 1

Theme from "The Fox" - 2 - 2

# SOPHISTICATED LADY

Words and Music by
DUKE ELLINGTON, IRVING MILLS
and MITCHELL PARISH

Sophisticated Lady - 3 - 1

# GET HAPPY

Words and Music by
HAROLD ARLEN and TED KOEHLER

Get Happy - 3 - 1

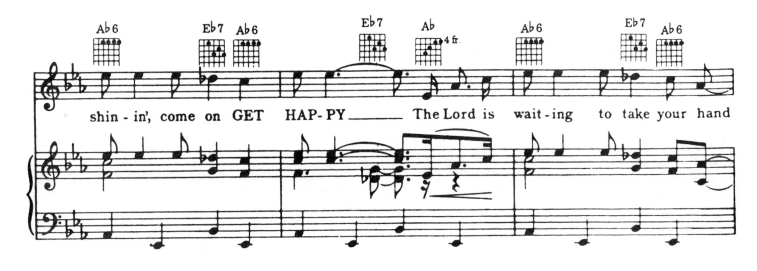

shin - in', come on GET HAP-PY _____ The Lord is wait-ing to take your hand

_____ _____ Shout Hal - le - lu - jah! come on, GET HAP-PY _____ We're go -

_ ing to the prom-ised land We're head - in'_'cross the Riv - er, wash your

# I GET A KICK OUT OF YOU

Words and Music by
COLE PORTER

I Get a Kick out of You - 4 - 1

REFRAIN

I Get a Kick out of You - 4 - 4

# STOMPIN' AT THE SAVOY

Lyric by
ANDY RAZAF

Music by
BENNY GOODMAN, CHICK WEBB and
EDGAR SAMPSON

Stompin' at the Savoy - 4 - 1

Stompin' at the Savoy - 4 - 4

# I GOT IT BAD
## (And That Ain't Good)

By
**DUKE ELLINGTON** and **PAUL WEBSTER**

The po-ets say that all who love are blind; But

I'm in love and I ___ know what time it is! ___ The

Good Book says "Go seek and ye shall find". Well,

I Got It Bad - 4 - 1

144

I Got It Bad - 4 - 4

# 'S WONDERFUL

Words and Music by
GEORGE GERSHWIN and IRA GERSHWIN

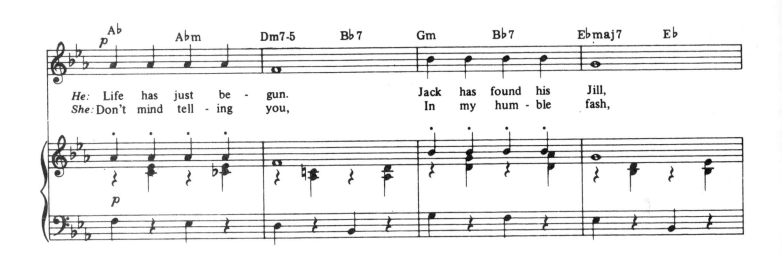

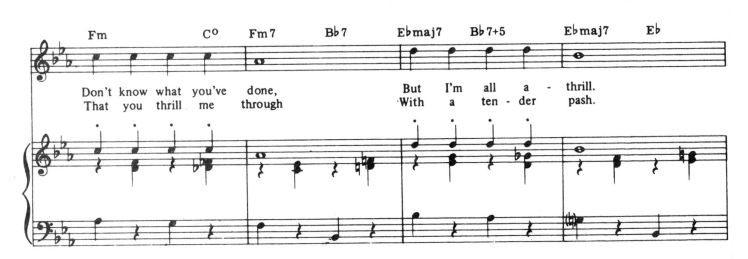

'S Wonderful - 4 - 1

148

# JERSEY BOUNCE

Words by
BUDDY FEYNE

Music by
BOBBY PLATER, TINY BRADSHAW
and EDWARD JOHNSON

Jersey Bounce - 2 - 1

# THE ODD COUPLE

Lyrics by
SAMMY CAHN

Music by
NEAL HEFTI

Moderato, Not too fast, with an insistent beat

The Odd Couple - 3 - 1

# JUMPIN' AT THE WOODSIDE

Words by
JON HENDRICKS

Music by
COUNT BASIE

156

Jumpin' at the Woodside - 3 - 2

Voices - I gotta go - I wanna blow
I gotta go - I wanna blow.
A little room - a lotta fun
I'm goin' home - I gotta run.
Jon - Not a little mansion an' it ain't
no motel.
I'm tellin' y' where the place is,
Bet - cha - never heard o' such a
groovy hotel.
Cop a room 'n then y' really c'n
Ten' t' biz.
Voices - I gotta go - I wanna blow
I gotta go - I got a really groovy pad
the better pad I ever had.
I gotta go - I wanna blow.
I gotta go - I never ever wanna move,
I never had a better groove.
I gotta go - I wanna blow
I gotta go - a tiny room is all I rent
But, man, I really do a lot o' livin'.
Piano - Eight bars
Voices - I gotta split - I gotta go
I'm gonna blow
Annie - That's it. - That's it. - That's it.
My hotel, - really glad I live at the woodside.
It's the greatest and grooviest pad that I've ever had,
An' I lived in lots of hotels
Everywhere from Bangor, Maine all the way to L.A.
When I hit the Woodside I settled down
An' I'm there to stay,
All day - all night there's bound to be
Somebody who has a horn,
Blowin', goin' on, sure's you're born,
Swingin' from mornin' till night.
When you're feelin' tight cool it.
Fall in the sleepers,
Sleep some - rest your peepers,
Then later, when you feel greater, dig -
Jon - Jumpin' in the hall 'n everybody has a ball.
'N what a ball - I do mean,
It's jumpin' every minute.
Soon - as - y' get inside the door
Well you can feel the shakin' floor
'N that alone'll tell y' th' hotel
Is quite a jumpin' scene.
Lower the blind - get outa your mind
On women 'n wine - y' try it.
You'll dig it.
I tell y' everybody has a ball in my hotel.
What a story I can tell
Y' finish up a gig' 'n tighten up your wig.

Y' never have t' wander aroun' 'n roam
You'll never find a groovier place
T' get the jumpin' really goin' on
You can make it in 'n have a ball at home.
Dig it - you'll find - it's swell.
I dig the Woodside - man, that's where I dwell.
I tell y' really, I'm livin'
'Cause I really have a ball in my hotel.
Voices - A lot o' jumpin' - y' dig it
Soon as you arrive.
A lot o' jumpin' - it's got another kind o' jive.
A lot o' jumpin' - n' really very much alive.
A lot - o' jumpin' - I tell y' sump'n, man,
They're jumpin'.
A lot o' jumpin' - at the Woodside now.
A lot o' jumpin' - y' cop a room 'n telephone.
A lot o' jumpin' - y' tell a fella' you're alone.
A lot o' jumpin' - n' you're no longer on your own.
A lot o' jumpin' - I tell y' sump'n, man,
They're jumpin' at the Woodside now.
A lot o' jumpin' - 'n you can do the way you please.
A lot o' jumpin' - they got a place where
You can grease.
A lot o' jumpin' - 'n you can live a life of ease.
A lot o' jumpin' - I tell y' sump'n, man,
They're jumpin' at the Woodside now.
A lot o' jumpin' - y' dig it comin' thru the door.
A lot o' jumpin' - n' you can feel the shakin' floor.
A lot o' jumpin' - 'n you'll be comin' back for more.
A lot o' jumpin' - I tell y' sump'n, man,
They're jumpin' at the Woodside now.
A lot of jumpin' - y' dig it soon as you arrive.
A lot o' jumpin' - 's got another kin' o' jive.
A lot o' jumpin' - 'n really very much alive.
A lot o' jumpin' - I tell y' sump'n, man,
They're jumpin' at the Woodside now.

# LI'L DARLIN'

By
NEAL HEFTI

# I GOT RHYTHM

Music and Lyrics by
GEORGE GERSHWIN and IRA GERSHWIN

I Got Rhythm - 4 - 1

162

REFRAIN *(with abandon)*

# NICE 'N' EASY

Words by
ALAN and MARILYN BERGMAN

Music by
LEW SPENCE

Nice 'N' Easy - 2 - 1

# IT'S ONLY A PAPER MOON

Words by
BILLY ROSE and
E. Y. HARBURG

Music by
HAROLD ARLEN

It's Only a Paper Moon - 4 - 3

# MY HEART STOOD STILL

*A Connecticut Yankee*

Words by
LORENZ HART

Music by
RICHARD RODGERS

*Martin:* I laughed at sweet - hearts
*Sandy:* Through all my school - days

I met at schools; All in - dis - creet hearts
I hat - ed boys; Those Ap - ril - Fool days

My Heart Stood Still - 4 - 1

# JUST ONE OF THOSE THINGS

Words and Music by
COLE PORTER

176

Just One of Those Things - 4 - 3

# LIZA
## (All the Clouds'll Roll Away)

Words by
IRA GERSHWIN and GUS KAHN

Words and Music by
GEORGE GERSHWIN

Liza - 4 - 1

whis - per sweet and low, That you ought to know, my Li - za!

I get lone - some, hon - ey, When I'm all a - lone so long;

Don't make me wait; Don't hes - i - tate; Come and hear my song:

Refrain
Li - za, Li - za, skies are gray,

180

Liza - 4 - 3

# THE MAN I LOVE

*French Version*
EMELIA RENAUD
*Spanish Version*
JOHNNIE CAMACHO

Words and Music by
GEORGE GERSHWIN and IRA GERSHWIN

The Man I Love - 4 - 1

184

# THE MAN THAT GOT AWAY

Words by
IRA GERSHWIN

Music by
HAROLD ARLEN

**Slowly** — *with a steady insistence*

The night is bit-ter, The stars have lost their glit-ter, The

winds grow cold-er And sud-den-ly you're old-er_ And all be-cause of the

man that got a - way,_____ No more his eag - er call;

The Man That Got Away - 4 - 1

The Man That Got Away - 4 - 2

The Man That Got Away - 4 - 4

*From "LAST TANGO IN PARIS"*

# LAST TANGO IN PARIS

Lyric by DORY PREVIN

Music by GATO BARBIERI

Last Tango In Paris - 3 - 1